CONTENTS

WHAT IS JAZZ?

"The closest thing I can get to saying what jazz is, is when you play what you feel. All jazz musicians express themselves through their instruments and they express the types of persons they are, the experiences they've had during the day, during the night before, during their lives."
(Jo Jones, quoted in *Hear Me Talkin' To Ya,* edited by Nat Shapiro and Nat Hentoff, Dover Publications, New York, 1955)

"The only form of art existing today in which there is freedom of the individual without the loss of group contact."
(Dave Brubeck, quoted in *Hear Me Talkin' To Ya*)

"Jazz is a form of art music which originated in the United States through the confrontation of blacks with European music."
(Joachim Berendt, *The Jazz Book*, Granada Publishing, 1983)

"Perhaps the most important music of the twentieth century." (John Storm Roberts, *Black Music of Two Worlds*, Praeger Publishers Inc., 1972)

"Afro-Classical music."
(Courtney Pine, quoted in *New Musical Express*, 18th October, 1986)

Some musicians, such as the trumpeter Miles Davis, have rejected the term "jazz" altogether, complaining that it is merely an invention of record companies anxious to label music. The term is useful, however, to distinguish certain styles of music which have their roots in a fusion of African and European traditions. These roots are examined in more detail in the next section.

Note on quotations
Unless stated otherwise, all quotations in this book are taken from *Hear me Talkin' To Ya.* This is a collection of extracts from magazine interviews with a host of jazz musicians and is well worth reading in its entirety.

Music Matters

JAZZ

Clive D. Griffin

Dryad Press Limited   London

Typeset by Tek-Art Ltd, Kent
and printed and bound by
Richard Clay Ltd,
Chichester, Sussex,
for the Publishers,
Dryad Press Limited,
8 Cavendish Square,
London W1M 0AJ

ISBN 0 8521 9754 3

ACKNOWLEDGMENTS

The Author and Publishers thank the following
for their kind permission to reproduce
copyright illustrations: BBC Hulton Picture
Library, pages 8, 10, 13, 17, 20, 23, 24, 26, 27,
28, 30, 31, 32, 34, 35, 37, 38, 39, 41, 44, 46, 59;
The Photo Source, pages 1, 6, 15, 19, 21, 22,
48, 49, 50, 52, 53, 54, 56. The map on page 61
is by R.F. Brien.

The cover photograph of Miles Davis is
reproduced courtesy of W.E.A. Records Ltd.

PART ONE

THE ROOTS OF JAZZ

===== AFRICAN MUSIC =====

"There is more of the sound of jazz in mid-European Gypsy fiddling than in a whole corps of African drummers." (Barry Ulanov, *A History Of Jazz In America*, Viking Press, New York, 1952)

This statement is often quoted as evidence of the lack of an African element in jazz. What it does highlight is the false impression that African music is nothing but drums. All African music contains certain common features and it was these features which were retained in the music of the Africans who were transported to the Americas during the years of the Slave Trade. The same features can be found in jazz.

Rhythm

The rhythms of African music are more complex than those of European music. Often several different rhythms are played at the same time. We use the word POLYRHYTHMIC to describe this. The same process occurs in jazz. The drums and bass set up a regular beat, but the other instruments cut across this, anticipating or delaying notes. Jazz musicians refer to this as "swinging". As the drummer Jo Jones put it, "Jazz has to swing. . . . The best way you can say what swinging is, is you either play with a feeling or you don't."

---

rhythm: *different combinations of stresses and sound lengths made into a pattern.*

---

beat: *a regular pulse.*

Instrumental tone

In European tradition, there tends to be an accepted "correct" tone for each instrument. African musicians are more concerned with finding an individual "voice".

"In Africa, music is not so much 'good' as 'effective', that is, right for its purpose." (John Storm Roberts, *Black Music Of Two Worlds*)

African musicians like to experiment with the possible sounds which can be obtained from instruments, and often use them to imitate the human voice. Jazz musicians have adopted a similar approach, using a variety of techniques to produce an individual tone.

Vocal tone

The comments about instrumental tone apply also to African singers. Singing and acting are seen as similar activities, and a "good" singer in Africa is one who can put on a suitable voice for the occasion. It is common practice for singers to "bend" notes or to slide up to the first note of a phrase. In jazz, this tradition continues in

---

tone: *This has two different meanings:*
(i) an interval of two semi-tones.
(ii) the quality of sound produced by an individual musician.
It is also used sometimes to mean TIMBRE. This is the sound produced by a particular instrument. (For example, the violin has a different timbre from the trumpet.)

A musician from Kinshasa in Zaire. String instruments of many different kinds are found throughout Africa.

the use of "blue notes", which will be discussed in more detail later.

Call and response

This is a vocal style found throughout Africa. One singer delivers a line, and an accompanying group of singers answers or repeats it. This technique appears in several different forms in jazz:

(a) A singer's phrase is "answered" by an instrumentalist. (See the later section on "Classic Blues".)

(b) A phrase played by one musician is answered by another. This is particularly true of the so-called "chase choruses". Here two musicians take it in turns to solo, each playing a four-bar phrase and trying to outdo the other. (This is also known as "trading fours".)

(c) Phrases played by one section of a big band are answered by another section. Alternatively, phrases played by a soloist are answered by the rest of the band. (See the later section on big bands.)

Improvisation

To improvise means to make something up as you go along. Improvisation occurs in both European and African music. In the time of Bach, for example, harpsichord players improvised harmonies around a given bass line. (This was known as "figured bass" or "basso continuo".) During this period (until about 1730), performers were also expected to improvise their own ornamentation ("fiddly bits"), but from the eighteenth century onwards, composers began to write in more detailed instructions as to how a piece was to be performed. In European music, improvisation gradually became less common. In African music, however, it continued to occupy a central place, with musicians, such as drummers, improvising around a "master pattern". The importance of improvisation in jazz, therefore, is more likely to be an African than a European influence.

Improvisation in jazz takes three main forms:

(a) "Individualizing" a melody through the use of ornamentation or the style of delivery.

(b) Using the basic chords of a tune to improvise new melodic lines. (This is the most common form. Jazz musicians refer to the chords of a tune as "the changes".)

(c) "Free" improvisation, in which the musicians make up the music as they go along, without using any pre-arranged chord pattern.

Audience participation

In traditional African music, there is no such thing as an audience that just sits still and listens. Music is a communal experience and everyone is expected to join in, by clapping or dancing or by taking part in call-and-response passages. This is also true of jazz, where even in a concert hall, members of the audience will tap their feet, call out encouragement and applaud individual soloists as they finish.

---

melody: *an arrangement of single notes. A tune.*

---

chord: *a group of three or more notes sounded together. The series of chords which accompanies a melody is known as a chord progression. It is possible to fit new melodies to such a series of chords.*

---

harmony: *a combination of musical sounds. The CHORDS which accompany a tune.*

---

bar: *a group of beats, the first of which is generally stressed (emphasized). The number of beats in a bar is indicated by the TIME SIGNATURE.*

Military bands

Military, or concert, bands differ from the brass bands found in Britain in that they contain both brass and woodwind instruments. Such bands originated in France during the nineteenth century, but also became very popular in the U.S.A. Their repertoire has always consisted mainly of transcriptions of light classical music and marches. So far as jazz is concerned, their influence has been in the tradition of combining brass and woodwind instruments and in the use of the march form.

transcription: *an arrangement of a piece of music for instruments other than those for which it was originally written.*

light classical: *popular classical music of the nineteenth century. For example, Rossini's William Tell overture or the waltzes of Johann Strauss.*

march: *a form of music, usually with four beats to the bar, originally written for military parades.*

Despite its association with jazz, the saxophone was first developed for use in military bands. As this picture shows, the instrument comes in many sizes.

The greatest composer of military band marches was the American, JOHN PHILIP SOUSA (1854-1932), who was known as "The March King". His compositions included "The Liberty Bell" and "The Washington Post". Such marches all had a similar pattern. First there was an eight-bar introduction. This was followed by two sixteen-bar themes and a trio section in a different key. The original themes were then repeated. Many early jazz numbers adopted a similar pattern. (See also the section on RAGTIME.)

---

key: *A piece of music is often said to be "in" a particular key. This means that the notes of the major or minor scale with that name will be used. The melody will generally finish on the starting note of that scale. Notes which do not belong to that scale can also be used, to add extra colour. They are known as CHROMATIC notes, after the Greek word for colour.*

During the nineteenth century, composers made increasing use of such notes. Their harmony was no longer based on major and minor scales and became known as CHROMATIC HARMONY.

During the twentieth century, a system was developed which gave all twelve notes of the chromatic scale equal importance, doing away with the idea of key altogether.

---

scale: *a set of notes, arranged in ascending order. The major and minor scales of Western music consist of eight notes. Whatever the starting note of the scale, the INTERVALS (distances) between each note and the next are the same. A chromatic scale consists of twelve notes, each a semi-tone from the next. These are not the only types of scale available. Many cultures, for example, make use of pentatonic scales, which have five notes.*

---

theme: *a short melody. The main musical idea of a piece, around which variations can be written or improvised.*

---

trio section: *a section in a piece of music written in a contrasting style and usually in a different key.*

Tin-pan alley

This phrase originally referred to a district in New York in which the composers and publishers of popular music had their headquarters. In the days before cassette recorders and demo-discs, composers had to impress publishers by sitting down at a piano and playing through their latest composition. Popular music therefore relied far more upon interesting melodies or unusual chord changes than it does nowadays. Such music was seized upon by jazz musicians as a basis for their own improvisations.

Like military band marches, popular music from the 1920s until the birth of Rock'n'Roll in the 'fifties tended to follow a regular pattern. First there came an introductory verse, usually sixteen bars long. This led into the main part of the song, the chorus. Choruses were generally thirty-two bars long, divided into four eight-bar sections. The first two were the same, while the third was in a different key. (This was known as "the bridge" or "the middle eight".) The fourth section was a repeat of the first. This is known as an AABA sequence.

The most influential composer of popular music, certainly so far as jazz is concerned, was GEORGE GERSHWIN (1898-1937). He was a brilliant pianist with a natural gift for improvisation. His songs were used extensively by jazz musicians and, in turn, he borrowed many ideas from jazz. He longed to be taken seriously as a composer and several of his works have become part of the classical repertoire. These include "Rhapsody In Blue", "An American In Paris" and his "Preludes" for piano. He is best-known, however, for his opera "Porgy and Bess". Although it is set in a black community in the southern United States (and Gershwin demanded that it always be performed by an all-black cast), the opera also displays Gershwin's New York Jewish background. "Summertime", perhaps the most popular song from the opera, combines elements of both black and Jewish music. Its melody

is very similar to that of a nineteenth-century Yiddish folk song, "Mayn Rue Plats" ("My Resting Place"). Such songs were performed by klezmer bands in Jewish districts of America in the early decades of this century. The development of klezmer music is very similar to that of jazz. In the nineteenth century wandering bands of Jewish musicians – klezmorim – travelled throughout eastern Europe playing at weddings and other celebrations. They mixed European dance tunes, marches and folk melodies with the ancient Middle Eastern music of their ancestors. A typical band might consist of cornet, clarinet and saxophone, augmented by violin, mandolin and tsimbalom (a large dulcimer played with small wooden hammers). Group improvisation was a feature of such bands. The music was taken to America by Jewish emigrants and a more direct jazz influence crept in. Some of the younger klezmer musicians found themselves work in goyishe jazz bands. It is worth noting here the number of white jazz musicians of the 'twenties and 'thirties who had a Jewish or eastern European background.

European classical music

The harmony of jazz is derived mainly from European classical music. Harmony means a combination of musical sounds produced at the same time. During the early seventeenth century in Europe a system of harmony was developed which was based on the major and minor scales. This is known as "diatonic harmony". Most well-known tunes – for example, "Happy Birthday to You", "God Save The Queen" and "The Red Flag" – use this system. New systems, for example "chromatic harmony" and "twelve-tone harmony", were developed during the nineteenth and twentieth centuries.

The earliest forms of jazz, in the 1920s and 1930s, relied on diatonic harmony – as does most popular music even today. From the 'forties onwards, however, jazz musicians became more and more interested in the modern developments which had taken place in European classical music.

> "I first began listening seven or eight years ago. First I heard Stravinsky's 'Firebird Suite'. . . . I guess Bartok has become my favourite."
> (Charlie Parker, one of the founders of modern jazz)

Many jazz musicians have studied European classical music at college. The trumpeter WYNTON MARSALIS is well-known equally for his jazz and for his classical performances – he has won awards for both. Jazz musicians have always searched for new ideas, new ways of expressing themselves. At this point it is worth referring back to Courtney Pine's definition of jazz – "Afro-Classical music."

Yiddish: *language spoken by Jews in central and eastern Europe, developed during the Middle Ages. It is a dialect of German with a sprinkling of Hebrew and Slavonic words.*

---

dulcimer: *a stringed instrument of the zither family, played with hammers rather than plucked.*

---

goyishe: *the Yiddish word for non-Jews (Gentiles).*

≣ AFRO-AMERICAN MUSIC ≣

Jazz was not the first form of music to mix African and European elements. Such mixing had taken place from the time that the first Africans were taken to the Americas. All the earlier types of Afro-American music influenced jazz, but two forms, BLUES and RAGTIME, made a more direct and substantial contribution.

Blues

Blues is the folk music of black Americans. The music grew out of an earlier form, FIELD HOLLERS. These were the improvised songs of people working on their own in the fields of the southern United States. Sometimes they were used as a way of passing messages from one field to another, but more often the singer was putting personal feelings into song. The use of falsetto singing was common, as were the bending and slurring of notes. These are both features of African music.

Towards the end of the nineteenth century, a more structured form of field holler developed. The name BLUES was given to this form of music early in the twentieth century. Blues retained many features of the holler – the bending and slurring of notes, the occasional use of falsetto, and lyrics which dealt with hardship, especially broken love affairs, without ever becoming self-pitying. The main difference was that, in place of the hollers' totally improvised melody lines, blues adopted a regular chord pattern.

This was based on the I, IV and V chords of European harmony and the most common pattern which emerged was the so-called twelve-bar blues. This consisted of four bars on I, two bars on IV, two on I, one on V, one on IV and two on I. In the key of C, for example, a simple twelve-bar blues would use the following chords:

```
C / / / C / / / C / / / C7 / / /
F / / / F / / / C / / / C / / /
G / / / F / / / C / / / C / / /
```

The first half of each line would be sung. The second half consisted of an instrumental "answer".

---

falsetto: *a register, available to adult voices, above the normal pitch.*

---

slur: *an unbroken move from one note to another.*

Jazz musicians have always made extensive use of this pattern as well as the thirty-two bar popular song sequence mentioned earlier. Often they will add extra "substitute" chords to the basic pattern, but the ability to play a slow blues has always been regarded as the hallmark of a good jazz musician.

A second feature of the blues which had an influence upon jazz was the use of "blue notes". These correspond to the third and seventh degrees of the European major scale. In the blues they are often flattened or bent. It is this which give the blues its peculiar haunting quality, with melodies which are neither totally in a major or in a minor key. In the key of C major, for example, the third degree of the scale is E. A blues musician might use E♭, which belongs to the key of C minor, or slur from E♭ to E.

Although they are called "blue" notes, the flattened third and seventh also occur in black music of South America and the Caribbean. This would suggest that they are a result of a fusion of African vocal techniques and European harmony. Since the 1940s, jazz musicians have also made great use of the flattened fifth, making this a third "blue note".

Ragtime

Ragtime was the immediate forerunner of jazz. Indeed, it is difficult to say where the one ends and the other begins. Ragtime began as piano music, but it was adapted to other instruments and small bands.

The style emerged around 1890 in the town of Sedalia, Missouri. Its leading practitioner and composer was the pianist, SCOTT JOPLIN, who had been born in Texas in 1868. Joplin's compositions closely followed the European military march form discussed earlier, but while the left-hand part consisted of a regular "oom-pah" figure, the right hand cut across this with syncopated melody lines. This became known as "ragged time", later shortened to "ragtime". Joplin wished to be taken

Scott Joplin.

---

syncopation: *placing an accent on the normally unstressed beats of a bar, or playing whole groups of notes which clash with the underlying beat.*

seriously as a composer in the traditional European sense. He insisted that his compositions be played exactly as written and particularly disliked the way in which so many ragtime pianists played everything quickly. Many of his rags were prefaced with the instruction "Not fast" or "Not too fast". In 1911, he even composed a ragtime opera, entitled "Treemonisha".

At the other extreme of ragtime was Ferdinand Joseph La Menthe, better known as JELLY ROLL MORTON. Born in Louisiana in 1885, he began his career playing piano in the "sporting houses" of New Orleans (more about these later). He blended ragtime with elements of the blues and of Latin American music. He was the first major ragtime pianist to move away from the tradition of composer-dominated music, improvising freely around his own, and other people's, tunes. His claim, "I invented jazz in 1902", is an exaggeration, but there was hardly a single jazz pianist in the 'twenties and 'thirties whose style did not owe something to Morton.

Latin American music: *Latin America refers to those parts of South America originally colonized by Spain or Portugal. Latin American music combines elements of Spanish, Portuguese and African music.*

PART TWO

FOUR CITIES

Jazz was not the product of one person or one place. The influences discussed in Part One were combined in various forms at the turn of the century throughout the United States. Having said this, however, four cities — NEW ORLEANS, CHICAGO, NEW YORK and KANSAS CITY — stand out as major centres in the development of jazz.

A street in one of the older parts of New Orleans.

New Orleans is popularly regarded as the birthplace of jazz. While this is not the complete truth, the city was certainly home to the majority of the great musicians in the first phase of jazz history, and the earliest style of jazz is still known as "New Orleans", wherever it is played. To understand this, it is necessary first to look at the geography and history of New Orleans.

The city stands on the Mississippi, about 172 km from the sea (the Gulf of Mexico). It is the second largest port in the U.S.A., and the Mississippi, along with its tributary, the Missouri, links New Orleans with the rest of the eastern United States. New Orleans was founded by the French in 1718, belonged to Spain from 1763, and was sold to the United States by France, during the Napoleonic wars, in 1803, as part of the "Louisiana Purchase".

At the beginning of the twentieth century, New Orleans was a melting-pot of different races and cultures. The French and Spanish inhabitants had been joined by immigrants from Britain and Italy. The black inhabitants of the city were divided into those who could trace their ancestry back to the French occupation – the Creoles – and those who had arrived later. Generally speaking, the Creoles made up the black middle class, the later arrivals the working class. Before 1865, the Creoles had privileges denied to other blacks, though after the Civil War and the abolition of slavery, these privileges ended. The Creoles looked towards France for their culture, and it is interesting to note the number of early jazz musicians with a Creole background – SYDNEY BECHET, JOE "KING" OLIVER, ALPHONSE PICOU, KID ORY, BUDDY PETIT, BARNEY BIGARD, FREDDIE KEPPARD and JELLY ROLL MORTON (Ferdinand Joseph La Menthe).

These racial and cultural differences were reflected in the music of New Orleans. This ranged from French ballet and military bands to the African dances peformed in the city's Congo Square. At the turn of the century, the city of 200,000 inhabitants had thirty dance bands (generally referred to as "orchestras") and an even larger number of marching bands. These marching bands performed at all sorts of open-air events – picnics, funerals and the New Orleans carnival, Mardi Gras. They included THE OLYMPIA BRASS BAND, THE RELIANCE BRASS BAND, THE ORIGINAL CREOLE BAND and THE EAGLE BAND.

Such bands were in the tradition of French military bands, but gradually, under the influence of black musicians, the "jazzing up" of tunes became common. The French style of the Creoles was modified by the African influence of New Orleans' black working class. This fusion was one of the main ingredients of New Orleans jazz.

According to tradition, the greatest band leader, and the first jazz musician, was BUDDY BOLDEN.

"I used to hear Bolden every chance I got . . . he'd put his horn out the window and blow, and everyone would come running."
(Kid Ory)

"They talk about Buddy Bolden – how, on some nights, you could hear his horn ten miles away."
(Danny Barker)

Mardi Gras: *the New Orleans carnival. It takes place on Shrove Tuesday, the day before Ash Wednesday. This is the start of the period of Lent, when Catholics traditionally give up the eating of meat. The word CARNIVAL comes from the Spanish for "farewell to flesh". Mardi Gras, the French for Shrove Tuesday, means literally "fat Tuesday", the last day for eating meat.*

---

horn: *in jazz, any brass or woodwind instrument is called a horn.*

The Olympia Brass Band. "Fats" Houston leads the funeral procession for veteran New Orleans trumpeter "Punch" Miller in 1971.

"Bolden was a strong trumpet player. You couldn't help from playing good with Bolden. He was crazy for wine and women and vice versa."
(Albert Gleny)

"The sad part is Buddy actually did go crazy a few years later and was put away in an insane asylum in Jackson, Mississippi. He was just a one-man genius that was way ahead of 'em all . . . too good for his time."
(Louis Armstrong)

Bolden did not make any records, so his reputation rests solely upon the recollections of other jazz musicians. We do know that he finally went insane, using his instrument as a weapon with which to beat other members of his band. Whether or not his playing could be heard ten miles away is open to question, but it is true that the leaders of the marching bands were all cornet or trumpet players and that loudness of tone was a principal requirement — remember, this was outdoor music.

"Battles" between rival bands were commonplace. When two bands met on the streets, each tried to outdo the other.

"Down the street, in an old sideboard wagon, would come the jazz band from one ballroom. And up the street, in another sideboard wagon, would come

17

the band from another ballroom, which had announced a dance for the same night at the same price. And those musicians played for all their worth, because the band that pleased the crowd more would be the one the whole crowd would go to hear, and dance to, at its ballroom later that night."
(Wingy Manone)

Even today, New Orleans-style trombone playing is known as "tailgate" because, when bands were pulled around on horse-drawn wagons, the trombone player had to sit at the back so that he could operate his slide over the tailgate of the wagon and not get in the way of the other musicians.

The marching bands were one ingredient of New Orleans jazz. The other main ingredient was the piano style which developed in the "sporting houses" of Storyville. Like all major ports, New Orleans had its "red-light" district – an area of bars, gambling dens and brothels. The Storyville district of New Orleans was named after SIDNEY STORY, the city councillor who drew up its boundaries in 1897.

"About the middle ways of the city of New Orleans . . . Canal Street was the dividing line between the uptown and the downtown section . . . and right behind Canal Street was Storyville . . . and right off Canal Street was the famous Basin Street . . . lots of prostitutes lived in different sections of the city and would come down to Storyville just like they had a job. . . . And business was so good in those days with the fleet of sailors and the crews from those big ships that come in the Mississippi River from all over the world."
(Louis Armstrong)

The "boss" of Storyville was a man called Tom Anderson. He published a "Blue Book", which was a guide to the district's brothels or "sporting houses":

"If there is anything new in the singing and dancing line that you would like to see while in Storyville, Piazza's is the place to visit, especially when one is out hopping with friends – the women in particular."

The most famous "house" was Mahogany Hall, at 235 Basin Street. A high-class brothel, this was run by a lady called Lulu White, and was immortalized in pianist Clarence Williams's "Mahogany Hall Stomp".

Each sporting house had its "professor", or piano player. These musicians played a mixture of ragtime and a blues-based style which later became known as "boogie-woogie". Both styles depended upon a regular left-hand part over which syncopated right-hand figures were played. The greatest of the professors was Jelly Roll Morton. As well as playing in New Orleans, he travelled to other parts of the United States, to places as far apart as Chicago and California. He took elements of the emerging New Orleans style with him, but also absorbed other influences while on his travels and brought them back to New Orleans.

Some of the larger sporting houses employed small bands, and there was also work for such bands on the riverboats which travelled up and down the Mississippi. In this way, the New Orleans style of playing was introduced to other towns. The man responsible for introducing jazz bands to the riverboats was Fate Marable. Marable employed many musicians who were later to become famous, among them LOUIS ARMSTRONG. Because of the high standards demanded by Fate Marable, musicians referred to gaining jobs in his riverboat bands as "going to the conservatory".

Gradually, the standard New Orleans band line-up emerged. The "front-line" instruments were cornet (or trumpet), clarinet and trombone. The rhythm section consisted of drums, banjo and tuba. Sometimes a piano would be added. The

conservatory: *a music school.*

The Mississippi linked New Orleans with other towns in the United States.

cornet generally took the lead, while the clarinet wove a counterpoint melody and the trombone added a tenor part. The banjo provided the basic chords, with the tuba playing a bass line and helping to emphasize the beat. The drums were played very much in the military band tradition, stressing the first and third beats of the bar, as in a march. The front-line instruments improvised around the chords and melodies of tunes, often ragtime numbers, and the emphasis was on collective, or group, improvisation rather than solo work.

Sometime around 1914, this style of music began to attract attention outside New Orleans. It was also at this time that the name "jazz" (or "jass") came into common use. (The word was black slang for energy, particularly of a sexual kind!) The first ever recordings of jazz were actually made by a white band, THE ORIGINAL DIXIELAND JAZZ BAND. In 1917, they recorded "Dixie Jass Band One-Step" and "Livery Stable Blues". The success of the ODJB was followed by the THE NEW ORLEANS RHYTHM KINGS, another white band. This white style of jazz is generally known as "Dixieland", whereas the black style is referred to as "New Orleans".

---

counterpoint: *a form of music in which two or more melodies sound at the same time. The horizontal movement of parts is more important than the vertical structure of chords.*

---

cornet: *often confused with the trumpet, it is actually a member of the horn family. It is smaller than the trumpet and has a more mellow timbre.*

---

tuba: *a general term for the bass members of the brass family. Jazz bands tended to use the Sousaphone, a large tuba that encircles the player's body and which has a bell that faces forward instead of upward. It was developed for use in the bands of John Philip Sousa.*

Dixieland: *the southern United States. The word possibly comes from a nickname for New Orleans, after a ten-dollar bill printed there (dix = ten in French).*

In 1917, the United States entered the First World War and Storyville was closed down on the orders of the Secretary of the Navy. He was worried that American sailors based in New Orleans might be led astray. Deprived of places to work, many jazz musicians moved north to Chicago.

◄ *The First recordings of jazz were made by white musicians who tended to emphasize the "novelty" elements of the music.*

San Jacinto Hall, New Orleans, once echoed to the sound of jazz bands.

Although the first style of jazz is still known as "New Orleans", wherever it is played, none of the earliest recordings of the music were actually made in that city. Most of them were made in Chicago, by musicians from New Orleans.

The development of jazz in the 1920s is closely linked with organized crime. It is no exaggeration to say that jazz musicians relied on gangsters as patrons, in the same way that classical composers of the seventeenth and eighteenth centuries relied on the aristocracy. In 1920, the United States government passed a law prohibiting the manufacture and sale of intoxicating liquor. Prohibition, as it was known, provided American gangsters with a golden opportunity. People still wanted alcohol, but as its production and distribution were illegal, the trade came under the control of criminal gangs led by men such as AL CAPONE. "Bootlegging" liquor was big business and bloody wars were fought between rival gang leaders anxious to have total control of this lucrative trade. Alcohol could not be sold openly but it was freely available in the illegal night-clubs or "speakeasies". No speakeasy was complete without a jazz band and there was plenty of work for musicians who were prepared to take the risks.

---

bootlegging: *The illegal production and sale of alcohol.*

Prohibition did not stop people drinking, but they had to do so in "speakeasies", illegal bars like the one pictured here.

"One night, a bunch of tough guys came in and started turning tables over to introduce themselves."
(Jimmy McPartland)

"We would see the rods coming up – and duck·"
(George Wettling)

"A frequent visitor to the Grand Terrace was the big man himself, Al Capone, who went around town in a seven-ton armored limousine. He liked to come into a club with his henchmen, order all the doors closed, and have the band play his requests."
(Earl Hines)

---

rods *guns.*

Al Capone (in the hat) was eventually arrested for tax evasion. He died in prison.

New Orleans in Chicago

The most important bandleader in Chicago in the early 'twenties was JOE "KING" OLIVER, whose CREOLE JAZZ BAND was the first black jazz band to be recorded. Born in 1885, Oliver had no formal musical training but learnt his trade in various marching bands, first on trombone then on cornet. He moved to Chicago in 1918 and became very popular. In 1922, he decided to add a second cornet player to his band. The musician he chose was to change the course of jazz history. LOUIS ARMSTRONG, also known as "SATCHMO" (satchel-mouth), was born in New Orleans in 1900. He had his first cornet lessons in an orphanage, to which he had been sent in 1913 after being arrested for firing a pistol in the street during the 1913 New Year's celebrations. He played in various marching bands – Kid Ory's and The Tuxedo Brass Band – and was also one of Fate Marable's riverboat musicians. When he arrived in Chicago, he soon made a name for himself. Other musicians admired him for his clarity of tone, his ability to play high notes (at that time top C was regarded as the upper limit by most cornet and trumpet players) and, above all, his powers of improvisation.

In 1924, Armstrong married LIL HARDIN, the pianist in the Creole Jazz Band. She persuaded him to leave Oliver and form bands of his own. The result was the "Hot Five" and "Hot Seven" recordings made between 1925 and 1930. These marked the artistic highpoint of the New Orleans style but also heralded its decline. New Orleans jazz relied on collective improvisation, but Armstrong was a

Louis Armstrong's Hot Five, with John St Cyr (banjo), Johnny Dodds (clarinet), Kid Ory (trombone) and Lillian Hardin Armstrong (piano).

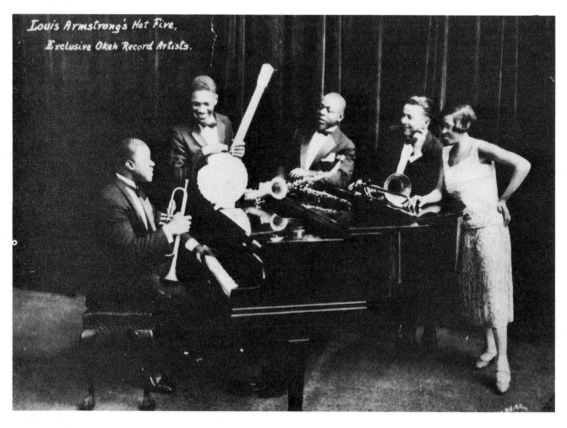

brilliant soloist who could not be confined within this format. His career marked the beginning of a change of emphasis in jazz, the era of the individual soloist. Ensemble passages were confined to the opening and closing choruses of tunes. Armstrong also broke away from the military band rhythms which had dominated jazz until that time. The older style can be described as "two beat" jazz, with the emphasis falling on the first and third beats of the bar. Armstrong was the first jazz musician to put the stress on all four beats of the bar.

Chicago Style

The music produced by black musicians in Chicago is generally known as "New Orleans In Chicago". There was another form of music to be found in the city, generally distinguished by the name "Chicago Style". Its originators were young white musicians who began by copying their black idols but who ended up producing something different. Chicago Style was also a form of two-beat jazz, but the emphasis was on the second and fourth beats of the bar (the "off-beats"). It was much more frantic than New Orleans jazz and, following the influence of Louis Armstrong, relied more on individual solos than on collective improvisation. Such bands also introduced the saxophone to jazz, sometimes in place of the trombone but more commonly as a fourth front-line instrument.

The greatest of the Chicago Style players, and perhaps the foremost white jazz musician ever, was BIX BEIDERBECKE.

---

ensemble: *a small group of musicians playing together.*

---

saxophone: *Invented by Adolphe Sax in the 1840s, the instrument was designed for use in military bands. It combined the characteristics of both brass and woodwind instruments. It comes in several sizes – soprano, alto, tenor, baritone and bass.*

He was born in 1903, in Davenport, Iowa, the son of German immigrants. His musical education started with piano lessons but, at the age of fourteen, he took up the cornet. According to legend, he was inspired to do this by the sound of the music coming from the Mississippi riverboats. He became totally absorbed in music – so much so that he was expelled from school.

In 1923, he joined THE WOLVERINES, the first of the Chicago Style bands. There followed periods with several other bands until 1927, when he joined the PAUL WHITEMAN ORCHESTRA. Whiteman led a dance band which borrowed elements from jazz – Gershwin's "Rhapsody in Blue" was originally written for the Whiteman orchestra. Many jazz fans could not understand why Beiderbecke joined such a band, but as well as jazz, he loved the orchestral compositions of Debussy and Ravel. He was fascinated by the lush arrangements which Whiteman used and, in turn, his cornet solos gave a touch of sharpness to the otherwise bland commercial sound of the orchestra.

Beiderbecke was noted for his beautiful tone, his sense of timing and the subtle nature of his improvised solos. Unfortunately, like so many great artists, he was destined for a tragic end. He was a perfectionist who was never entirely happy with his work and those who knew him felt that this was the reason for his heavy drinking. He suffered from a series of alcohol-related illnesses and died in August, 1931.

Classic Blues

In the section on "The Roots of Jazz", the blues was discussed as one of the forms of music which influenced jazz. Although the blues and jazz developed separately, Chicago in the 1920s saw a fusion of the styles, which came to be known as "Classic Blues". This was a city form of the old rural blues, and its greatest exponents were all women, usually accompanied by

Bix Beiderbecke. Probably the greatest of all white jazz musicians, he died at the age of only 28.

a small jazz band. Classic Blues recordings provide one of the finest examples of the use of call-and-response style in Afro-American music. Each line of the singer is answered by an improvised instrumental passage, or obligato. Much of Louis Armstrong's most inventive work can be found in such recordings.

The best-known of all the Classic Blues singers was BESSIE SMITH. In 1912, at the age of seventeen, she began touring with a travelling variety show whose line-up included another great female blues singer, MA RAINEY. By 1919, she was starring in her own shows. Her recording career began in 1923 and soon there were virtual riots at record shops as fans rushed to obtain her latest releases. She became known as the "Empress of the Blues" and the emotional impact of her performances was heightened by the hardships of her personal life.

"This was no actress; no imitator of woman's woes; there was no pretence. It was the real thing."
(Carl Van Vechten)

Bessie Smith recorded with many of the best jazz musicians of the day. Apart from Louis Armstrong, she worked with the pianist JAMES P. JOHNSON, trombonist JACK TEAGARDEN and the saxophone player, CHU BERRY. Armstrong said of her:

"She had music in her soul and felt everything she did."
(Quoted in *The Jazz Book* by Joachim E. Berendt, Granada Publishing, 1983)

She died in Mississippi in 1937, killed in a car crash. Although there is some dispute about the matter, it would seem that she was not taken to the nearest hospital along with the white victims of the crash. Instead, she was taken to a blacks-only hospital, further away, where she died from her injuries.

Bessie Smith, the "Empress of The Blues".

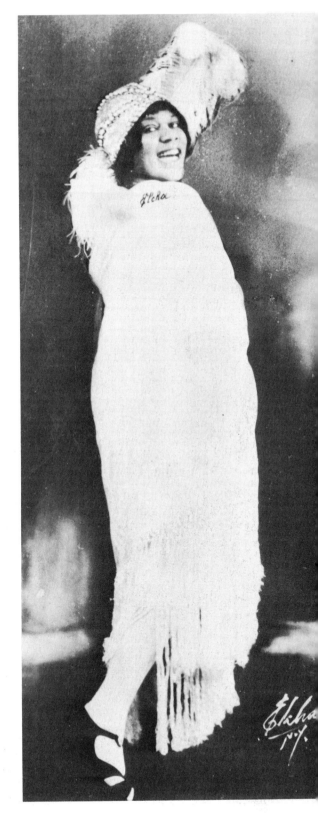

NEW YORK

In the first decades of this century, New York was the undisputed capital of American popular music. It was here that the record companies and the music publishers had their headquarters. Following the success of the Original Dixieland Jazz Band in 1917 (when their recording of "Livery Stable Blues" sold over three million copies), the entertainment industry began to see the commercial possiblities of jazz. As Chicago declined as a jazz centre, towards the end of the 'twenties, dozens of musicians moved to New York. The Harlem district of the city had the world's largest black urban population outside Africa. In the 'twenties and 'thirties it was a centre for black writers and political activists as well as musicians. It was here that a new style of jazz developed. It differed from New Orleans jazz in several ways:

(a) The trumpet gradually replaced the

Trumpeter Cootie Williams entertains the crowd at the Savoy Ballroom in Harlem, in the 1930s.

cornet as a front-line instrument, while the clarinet largely gave way to the saxophone. In the rhythm section, the role of the tuba was taken over by the more versatile string bass and the banjo was abandoned in favour of the guitar. The piano took a far more important role.

(b) The bands gradually became larger, with instruments arranged into sections.

(c) "Two-beat" jazz was replaced by "four-beat" jazz – the beginning of the style known as Swing. (The word "swing" has two meanings. It refers to the attitude towards rhythm shared by all jazz musicians and also to the big band style of the 'thirties. Usually, the latter meaning is indicated by the use of a capital S.)

The big band phase of jazz began with a musician called FLETCHER HENDERSON. He led a band at Harlem's Roseland Ballroom, as early as 1919. With a line-up of nine or ten musicians, it was not much bigger than the New Orleans bands. The important difference was that Henderson started grouping the instruments in sections and wrote out arrangements for these sections to play, over which soloists could improvise. The soloists who were drawn to Henderson's bands included Louis Armstrong and the first great tenor saxophone player, COLEMAN HAWKINS. In the early days of jazz, the music was dominated by trumpet players. After Hawkins, the saxophone, particularly the tenor sax, challenged this supremacy. The instrument allows musicians great variety of tone, and many of the most distinctive "voices" of jazz have been saxophonists.

Henderson's musical arrangements, simple as they now sound, marked a turning point in jazz. Earlier styles had relied on "head arrangements" – agreed on verbally by the musicians. The big band style used a combination of written arrangements and improvised solos. The greatest exponent of this form of music was DUKE ELLINGTON.

Jazz bands often described themselves as "orchestras", but Ellington's was one of the few in which the different instruments were used in an orchestral manner. Edward Kennedy Ellington was born in Washington D.C. in 1899. His first ambition was to be a painter, and although he abandoned this for music, he used sound in the way that an artist uses colour. The strength of his arrangements was that he wrote for the individual musicians in his orchestra, not just for instruments. He knew the strengths of his musicians and their individual voices. As a result, Ellington arrangements only sounded at their best when played by the Ellington orchestra. It was a sound that was impossible to copy, though many tried. It was rightly said of him that although he played the piano, his true instrument was the band.

In 1923, Ellington made his first visit to New York, with a five-piece band called THE WASHINGTONIANS. After six months of near starvation, the musicians gave up. Three years later, Ellington returned to work at Harlem's most famous night-spot, THE COTTON CLUB. At the time he was actually under contract to a theatre in Philadelphia, but the manager was "persuaded" to release him. Gangsters were the real owners of many of New York's nightclubs. When The Plantation Club was opened as a rival to The Cotton Club it was wrecked after only two nights and its owner murdered.

Although it was situated in Harlem, The Cotton Club operated a whites-only policy as far as its audience was concerned. (Black people were, however, allowed to serve drinks and provide music.) The aim of the club was to give white tourists the feeling that they had really been to Harlem. The management pandered to the ignorance and prejudice of their customers and the emphasis was upon the supposedly "primitive" background of black Americans. The Ellington band was required to produce so-called "jungle style" music. Ellington turned this to his advantage and wrote some of his finest compositions for The Cotton Club orchestra.

New Year's Eve at The Cotton Club, 1937. The bandleader is Cab Calloway.

mute: *a device placed in the bell of a brass instrument to alter its tone. Early jazz musicians used a variety of home-made mutes, ranging from empty bottles to bowler hats.*

His most important soloists were the trombonist JOE "TRICKY SAM" NANTON and the trumpeter BUBBER MILEY. They were masters of the "plunger" mute. Originally this was nothing more sophisticated than a rubber sink-plunger with the handle removed. By holding it in front of the bell of a trumpet or trombone and either moving it away slightly or squeezing it, it was possible to achieve a variety of different tones. Nanton and Miley were so skilled that they could almost make their instruments talk. This style can be heard at its most expressive in one of Ellington's best-known compositions, "Black and Tan Fantasy".

In later years, Ellington was to develop other styles. The "mood style", heard in such pieces as "Mood Indigo" and "Solitude", was heavily influenced by the blues. He also wrote music in the style of such popular composers as Cole Porter and Irving Berlin. In the late 'thirties, Ellington began to produce extended compositions. These ranged from pieces featuring individual members of the orchestra — "Concerto For Cootie", for example, was written for trumpeter COOTIE WILLIAMS — to large-scale works such as "Such Sweet Thunder". Composed in 1957, the latter was a series of musical portraits of Shakespearean characters.

The influence of the Ellington orchestra has been a constant feature of jazz since the late 'thirties. Ellington himself died on 25th May, 1974, in New York. In his lifetime, he did more than any other musician to destroy the myth that jazz is somehow inferior to other forms of music.

Duke Ellington and his orchestra in 1934.

"In those years around 1930, Kaycee was really jumping . . . at this time, which was still Prohibition, Kansas City was still under Tom Pendergast's control. Most of the night spots were run by politicians and hoodlums, and the town was wide open for drinking, gambling, and pretty much every form of vice. Naturally, work was plentiful for musicians, though some of the employers were tough people."
(Mary Lou Williams)

Kansas City produced more great jazz musicians than any other place in America. Some were born in the city, but the majority migrated there, attracted by the plentiful work and the musical atmosphere. The city was run by a gangster named Tom Pendergast and, as he had the local police and politicians under his control, Prohibition had little effect. Every night club and bar had a pianist or a small band and the music did not stop at closing time. After their regular paid employment had ended, musicians would get together for "jam sessions", playing just for the fun of it. Kansas City jam sessions were legendary, often going on for hours. They provided an opportunity for musicians to try out new ideas and for newcomers to show what they could do.

Kaycee: *Kansas City. In fact, there are two places called Kansas City, separated by the Missouri river. "Kansas City, Missouri, wasn't too prejudiced for a Midwestern town. It was a ballin' town, and it attracted musicians from all over. . . . Kansas City, Kansas, was right across the viaduct, just about five or six miles distant. But on the Kansas side they were much snootier." (Mary Lou Williams)*

◄ *Mary Lou Williams. One of the great Kansas City pianists, she was also in demand as an arranger and bandleader.*

Visiting jazz stars were expected to take part in these jam sessions and they often came off worst. The most famous casualty was Coleman Hawkins. He had arrived in Kansas City one day in 1934, with Fletcher Henderson, and after the band had finished its engagement he went along to a jam session at a club called The Cherry Blossom. Word went round that Hawkins was playing and, within an hour, the city's best tenor saxophonists, among them LESTER YOUNG, BEN WEBSTER and HERSCHEL EVANS, were all present. The pianist MARY LOU WILLIAMS tells how she was woken at about four in the morning by a knocking on her window. It was Ben Webster, who told her, "Get up, pussycat, we're jammin' and all the pianists are tired out now. Hawkins has got his shirt off and is still blowing. You got to come down."

The session went on all night and late into the next morning. Hawkins finally gave up, accepting that he could not better the Kansas City tenor players. He was due to be playing with Henderson in St Louis that night and legend has it that he ruined a brand new Cadillac trying to get there on time.

The music of Kansas City was firmly rooted in a hard, driving form of the blues. Like their counterparts in New Orleans and Chicago, Kaycee musicians relied upon "head arrangements". The bands of BENNIE MOTEN and COUNT BASIE developed the "riff style", employing two musical techniques which can be traced back to African music. The first is the repetition of short rhythmic phrases ("riffs"), the second is the use of call-and-response style. The different sections of the bands – trumpets, trombones and saxes – would "swap" riffs, developing a tremendous feeling of movement. Kansas City rhythm sections included such fine pianists as Count Basie, Mary Lou Williams and PETE JOHNSON. Johnson is also famous for his work with the blues singer JOE TURNER. Turner was the bar-tender at a club called The Sunset and would sing while serving drinks.

Count Basie and his band in 1944.

Among all the fine musicians who emerged from Kansas City, two in particular stand out – LESTER YOUNG and CHARLIE PARKER. Between them, "PRES" and "BIRD" dominated the jazz world for over thirty years. Jazz musicians are still described in terms of the influence Young or Parker has on their style.

Lester Young was born in Woodville, Mississippi, in 1909. He played the drums in a band made up of other members of his family, not taking up the tenor saxophone until he was in his twenties. In the 1930s he moved to Kansas City, playing with both Bennie Moten and Count Basie. For a while, he took Coleman Hawkins' place in Fletcher Henderson's band, before beginning another spell with Count Basie in 1936. He stayed with Basie for four years, during which time he also recorded with small groups and with the singer BILLIE HOLIDAY. It was she who gave Young the nickname "Pres" (short for president), while he referred to her as "Lady Day".

After leading small groups of his own, he joined Basie yet again in 1943. Young's

34

tenor style was in marked contrast to that of Hawkins. He employed a soft tone, with hardly any vibrato, and was a great influence on what came to be known as "cool jazz" (see Part Four). Hawkins once teased Young, saying that he should switch to alto sax as it would be more suited to his tone. Young replied that his music came from his brain, unlike other tenor players who were "all belly". When improvising on a melody, Young would

---

vibrato: *a slight, rapid alteration in the pitch of a note. A kind of controlled "wobble".*

Kansas City's two greatest sax players on stage together in 1949. Lester Young is on the left, Charlie Parker on the right. The pianist is Lennie Tristano.

always keep his mind on the lyrics which went with it. JO JONES, the drummer in the Basie band, described how Young would "literally talk on his horn".

In 1944, Pres began a disastrous spell in the U.S. Army. He had always been an individual character and found it difficult to conform. His army career ended with court martial and a year's detention. Always a gentle man, he emerged bitter and broken. He began drinking heavily and for years was almost permanently drunk. Between 1945 and 1959 he was never in good health and his playing suffered, only occasionally showing flashes of brilliance. In March, 1959, he was in Paris for an engagement at The Blue Note Club when he was taken ill. He insisted on returning to New York, where he died on the morning of his arrival.

Charlie Parker's early life displayed the other side of the free-and-easy atmosphere of Kansas City. Born in the city in 1920, he was using heroin by the age of fifteen and before he was twenty had already been married and divorced. Parker, nicknamed "Yardbird" or just "Bird", was one of the few musicians to whom the term "natural genius" can justly be applied. Before he was old enough to enter clubs legally, he would sneak in to watch his idol, Lester Young. The style he was to develop was based on Young's solos, but played at great speed on the alto sax. When he got his first instrument, he locked himself away for hours, teaching himself to play blues tunes in all twelve keys. If he had not been self-taught, he would have been told that jazz musicians only used a few of these keys regularly. His "mistake", however, meant that he developed incredible technical ability.

When he began taking part in jam sessions during the 'thirties, other musicians were impressed by this technique but less keen on the new ideas he wanted to try out. At that time, Parker's ideas often ran ahead of his abilities and there is a famous story about one particular jam session when the drummer, Jo Jones, threw a cymbal at him because he disliked what he was playing.

In 1937, Bird joined JAY McSHANN's band, a typical Kansas City blues-based outfit. In 1941, the band had an engagement at the Savoy Ballroom in Harlem. In New York, Parker discovered other musicians who were trying to find new ways of playing. Bored with playing stereotyped arrangements, he left McShann and started attending the jam sessions at a club called MINTON'S PLAYHOUSE in Harlem. It was here that the style known as "be-bop" was born. This is discussed in more detail in Part Four.

The impact of Charlie Parker on the development of modern jazz was as important as that of Louis Armstrong on more traditional forms of the music. The similarity ends there. Armstrong went on to become a popular all-round entertainer, "the ambassador of jazz". Although already twenty when Parker was born, he outlived him by sixteen years. Despite misguided attempts by many admirers to romanticize it, Parker's personal life was a mess. In 1946, he suffered a major breakdown, starting a fire in his hotel room and running naked into the corridor. In the "Lover Man" recording, made at the time, Parker was barely able to stand and the sound of his sax can be heard fading as he reeled away from the mike. He spent periods of time sleeping rough and would often stay awake all night, riding round and round on subway trains.

Towards the end of his life, his unpredictable behaviour led to his being barred from BIRDLAND, the New York jazz club named after him. In an attempt to keep away from hard drugs, he turned instead to drink. He died on 12th March, 1955. The doctor who performed the autopsy guessed his age as fifty-five — twenty years older than he really was.

PART THREE

THE SWING ERA

In 1933, Prohibition was repealed. The night clubs and bars in which jazz had flourished now became legal and jazz musicians were no longer dependent upon gangsters and hoodlums. Big band jazz emerged from the speakeasies and into the ballrooms. This change coincided with the end of the worst years of the period of extreme financial hardship known as the Depression. Young white high school and college students, looking for a style they could call their own, turned to the music, dancing and fashions of black America.

The Depression: *the period following the collapse of the American stock market in 1929 (The Wall Street Crash). Share prices fell, banks ran out of money, factories closed down and wages were cut. There was mass unemployment. Country areas were particularly badly hit. Banks insisted on loans being paid up at once, and thousands of farmers went bankrupt.*

In the 'thirties, jazz moved out of the "speakeasies" and into the ballrooms.

The jazz expression "swing" was adopted to describe this life-style. In many ways, this was a taste of what was to come in the Rock'n'Roll years of the 'fifties. As in the 'fifties, it was white musicians who became the big stars and who enjoyed commercial success.

The hero of this new jazz audience was the clarinettist, BENNY GOODMAN, the so-called "King of Swing". Born in Chicago in 1909, he learnt to play the clarinet in a synagogue youth band. He went on to play in a number of Chicago Style jazz bands, before moving to New York in 1928. In 1934, he formed his own big band and was as surprised as anyone by the enthusiasm with which it was received. Other white bandleaders who enjoyed the same sort of success as Goodman were the DORSEY BROTHERS, ARTIE SHAW and WOODY HERMAN. Jimmy and Tommy Dorsey were the children of Irish immigrant parents. Their father, a Pennsylvania coal-miner, also gave music lessons. He wanted his sons to have the musical career he had been denied and, in order to make sure that they stayed at home to practise, he hid their shoes. Jimmy played the alto sax, while Tommy was a trombonist. By the 1920s, the brothers were playing with the famous white dance bands of the period, including Paul Whiteman's. They were constantly arguing with each other and finally separated, each to lead his own big band.

The music of the white big bands grew from earlier jazz traditions, but the emphasis was often upon surface excitement rather than real feeling. Soloists such as the trumpeter HARRY JAMES or the drummer GENE KRUPA, both of whom played in the Goodman orchestra, were noted for their displays of technical brilliance and their crowd-pleasing solos. The arrangements written for the bands were higly polished, but left little room for improvisation. The extreme form of this was the music of the GLEN MILLER orchestra, which, whatever its merits, had a very limited jazz element.

The Glen Miller Orchestra representing big band music at its smoothest.

Sedate dances such as the foxtrot were replaced by the jitterbug and the lindy hop.

The true home of big band jazz was the ballrooms of the period. The Palladium Ballroom in Hollywood had space for 6,500 dancers, while New York's Roseland had a ceiling decorated with electric stars and walls covered in mirrors. More romantic was The Glen Island Casino, situated on a small island near New York. At night, the moon would shine off the water of Long Island Sound and through the windows of the ballroom. The Terrace Room of the New Yorker Hotel had an ice-rink which slid under the bandstand to reveal a dance-floor.

The patrons of these ballrooms had traditionally danced the foxtrot, a simple, sedate shuffle. The new, younger audiences, however, wanted something more lively and they turned to the dances of their black counterparts for inspiration. THE LINDY HOP and THE JITTERBUG were both athletic dances – forerunners of the 'fifties' JIVING – which involved swinging partners around and fancy footwork. THE BIG APPLE was so energetic that many ballrooms

banned it. It was performed by groups of eight to ten dancers and soon dissolved into a circle of flying arms and feet. KICKING THE MULE involved leapfrogging over your partner, while in BACK TO THE CIRCLE SWING one dancer would perform in the centre of a circle of encouraging friends. Dancing was such a part of the Swing era that even when bands played in theatres, the aisles became dance-floors.

Radio was still a new invention at this time, and radio stations were quick to jump onto the Swing bandwaggon. Disc jockeys became national celebrities, as important to musicians as to fans. The juke-box was another development which spread the impact of Swing. By 1939, there were 225,000 juke-boxes in the United States, using 13 million records a year. There was also an early version of the video-juke-box, known as the "soundy", which showed a short film to accompany the record. During the Swing era, the U.S. record business grew into a huge industry. Bands also made their music known by undertaking gruelling tours of one-night stands. Often the overnight journey was over three hundred miles. Bands would arrive in a new town late in the afternoon, grab a quick meal, test the sound equipment at the ballroom in which they were playing, change into their stage clothes and be on the bandstand by early evening. Musicians spent much of their lives on the band bus. Gambling was a constant pastime. In her book, *Lady Sings The Blues*, the singer Billie Holiday tells how she won sixteen hundred dollars from other members of the Basie band on one twelve-hour journey.

For black bands, the hardships of life on the road were increased by the racism they encountered, particularly in the southern states. Racial segregation was common in many areas and finding accommodation was always a problem. There were several attempts to build racially integrated bands, but the black musicians involved often suffered humiliation. The trumpeter, ROY ELDRIDGE, said that he would never work with a white band again after his experiences when working with Gene Krupa and Artie Shaw. He had nothing but praise for the other members of the Krupa band, but found that he was never allowed to stay in the same hotel as them. When he was with Artie Shaw, he was actually refused entrance to a ballroom, despite the fact that his name was up in lights over the door.

Many other musicians had tales to tell about conditions they encountered:

Edmond Hall said
"The furthest South we played . . . was Birmingham, Alabama. When we played there they had a rope right down the middle of the floor. There was white on one side and coloured on the other." (Edmond Hall)

"The one-night scene in the South was just simply terrible . . . sometimes we couldn't get off the stand for a drink of water unless we had a police escort." (Milt Hinton)

Although the 'thirties was the era of the big bands, it was also a time when the

Billie Holiday, the greatest singer of the Swing ▶ *era. She could perform popular songs of the day with all the emotional intensity of the great blues singers.*

---

juke-box: *The name originally comes from black American slang for a brothel – a "juke joint" or "juke house".*

---

segregation: *the separation of people according to the colour of their skin or their racial origins. In America, many states had "Jim Crow" laws which were similar to the apartheid policies of South Africa. The Civil Rights movement of the 'sixties was a campaign against this injustice.*

greatest jazz soloists emerged. The band arrangements provided a background against which these soloists could improvise. Some of them were figures from the early days of jazz – Louis Armstrong and Coleman Hawkins, for example. Others, such as Lester Young and Ben Webster, came to fame during the Swing era. A third group, among them Charlie Parker and the trumpeter DIZZY GILLESPIE, were to change the course of jazz over the next decade. The strength of the big bands was that they provided an environment in which such vastly different musicians could play.

Big bands were a regular source of employment for musicians and gave them a degree of financial security. This enabled them to pursue their own ideas in jam sessions, or in recording dates with small groups, made up of musicians from different bands. Many of the great soloists of the period also worked with such small groups.

The 'thirties was a period in which big band jazz and popular music were one and the same thing. This situation was not to last, however. Keeping a big band on the road was an expensive business and the entry of the United States into the Second World War in 1941 was the final straw for all but the most successful of them. Many musicians were drafted into the army and a heavy petrol tax, introduced as a wartime measure, made touring difficult. In addition to this, many younger musicians were becoming bored with the constraints of working in a big band, especially as more and more band leaders were more interested in following successful trends than in encouraging new ideas. By the time the war was over, the big band era had ended and "modern jazz" had arrived.

PART FOUR

MODERN JAZZ

Be-bop

"Some of us began to jam at Minton's in Harlem in the early 'forties. But there were always some cats showing up there who couldn't blow at all but would take six or seven choruses to prove it.

"So on afternoons before a session, Thelonious Monk and I began to work out some complex variations on chords and the like, and we used them at night to scare away the no-talent guys."
(Dizzy Gillespie)

Modern jazz did not begin in any one place – young musicians all over the United States were developing new ideas – but Minton's Playhouse in New York provided an environment in which these different experiments could be put together.

The music policy at Minton's was the brainchild of an ex-bandleader called TEDDY HILL. Instead of employing a regular band, he engaged a drummer and a pianist and invited other musicians to come and jam with them. The drummer was KENNY CLARKE, who had previously been sacked from Hill's own band because he did not play in a conventional Swing style. Instead of keeping the beat on his bass drum, he used his top cymbal, playing short rhythmic figures on the bass drum. Hill referred to this as "klook-mop stuff", gaining Clarke his nickname "Klook". The pianist, THELONIOUS MONK, had an equally unorthodox style. He used discordant harmonies and his playing had a jerky quality, as if he were selecting each chord before he played it. Clarke and Monk formed a rhythm section very different from that found in most big bands and musicians flocked to play with them.

JOHN "DIZZY" GILLESPIE was playing at the time with CAB CALLOWAY'S band. Another member of the band, DANNY BARKER, told of the problems Gillespie had:

"Cab would stop after a number sometimes, and if the arrangement had been changed, he would say: 'Whoever is doing that, the so-and-so should stop it. And you,' he would point to Dizzy,'I don't want you playing that Chinese music in my band.'"

Another musician who began playing regularly at Minton's was Charlie Parker. He and Gillespie are generally regarded as the two most important figures in the style which became known as "be-bop", or just "bop".

The main characteristic of this style was the way that melodies were broken down to their bare essentials. It was tense music, generally played at high speed. The musicians explored harmonies not previously used in jazz, breaking tunes apart and rebuilding them into something different. A common technique was to take the chords of a tune and use them to create a new melody (thus avoiding copyright). This melody would be played in unison first, then used as the basis for individual solos.

---

be-bop: *The name came from an attempt to imitate verbally the rhythm of this music. (See also "klook mop".)*

---

copyright: *In music, copyright law applies to melodies but not their underlying chord pattern.*

---

unison: *several musicians playing the same tune together, without using harmony.*

Dizzy Gillespie. At a party, someone once sat on his trumpet and bent it. After his initial anger had subsided, he found that he preferred the sound that it made in its new shape. He later discovered that a manufacturer had already patented a similar design and Gillespie has used such an instrument ever since.

Bop musicians did not advance only the harmonic theories used in jazz. Conventional ideas about rhythm were also challenged. Drummers were given a far more flexible role, while the task of keeping a regular beat was handed on to bass players. At the same time, however, bassists such as OSCAR PETTIFORD, RAY BROWN and CHARLES MINGUS had the technical ability to make the bass a solo instrument, as well as providing a rhythmic foundation. Drummers began to pay more attention to the melodic lines being played by other musicians, accompanying them rather than merely providing an even beat. It became common for drummers to be able to play other instruments and to know how to make arrangements.

The other two members of the rhythm section, the piano and the guitar, were also freed from their role of emphasizing the rhythm and harmony. They continued to do this, of course, but also became "front-line" instruments. The modern style of jazz piano playing can be traced back to EARL HINES, a contemporary of Louis Armstrong. He developed what became known as "trumpet style piano", in which the right hand played melodic lines in the manner of a trumpet or saxophone. BUD POWELL extended Hines's ideas and has been referred to as the Charlie Parker of the piano. At the same time as these developments were taking place, horn players were becoming more aware of the rhythmic function of their playing. Thus the distinction between rhythm-section and front-line instruments, which had been so rigid in New Orleans jazz, became blurred in be-bop.

Dizzy Gillespie was deeply interested in the rhythmic possibilities of this new style of jazz. He was fascinated by Afro-Cuban rhythms and played with musicians from the Cuban band led by MACHITO. The results were known as "Cu-Bop". He added a Cuban drummer, CHANO POZO, to this band in 1947. If Charlie Parker was the supreme musical genius of bop, it was Gillespie who popularized the music. His beret, goatee beard and dark glasses became as much a part of bop as the music. Be-bop became a social as well as a musical force, attracting those who disliked the commercialism of the Swing era. Bop musicians and fans had their own secret language – much of which was adopted by white teenagers during the 'fifties. They were hip cats who flipped their wigs over this crazy jive, snat-o-roonie. This language can be heard at its most extreme in the songs recorded by the pianist SLIM GAILLARD.

Much attention – too much perhaps – focused on the self-destructive life-styles of many bop musicians. The fate of Charlie Parker has already been mentioned, but his was not an isolated case. Bud Powell died in 1966, having spent much of his life since the early 'forties in psychiatric hospitals. The trumpeter FATS NAVARRO was a heroin addict who died of T.B. at the age of only twenty-six. Many others struggled with a drug habit. There was a foolish tendency to link the artistic achievements of these musicians with their life-styles – to play like Bird you had to live like him. Parker himself certainly did not go along with this idea:

"Any musician who says he is playing better either on tea, the needle, or when he is juiced, is a plain, straight liar. When I get too much to drink, I can't even finger well, let alone play decent ideas. And, in the days when I was on the stuff, I may have thought I was playing better, but listening to some of the records now, I know I wasn't."

Charlie Parker – "Bird".

It would be wrong to assume that be-bop replaced other forms of jazz. Many bop musicians continued to play in big bands as well as working with their own small groups. After being sacked by Cab Calloway, Dizzy Gillespie worked for various bandleaders, including Earl Hines and Duke Ellington. Charlie Parker also played for Earl Hines in 1943. Parker disliked big band work, but Gillespie enjoyed it. As well as playing in a quartet with Parker, he formed a series of big bands of his own, taking one of them to Europe in 1948.

During the 'forties and 'fifties, the promoter NORMAN GRANZ put together a series of touring packages known as JAZZ AT THE PHILHARMONIC. Granz's idea was to re-create the excitement of the jam session in a concert hall. Rather than booking bands, he engaged individual musicians whom he thought would play well together. These included soloists from the Swing era as well as be-boppers. JATP regulars included Lester Young, Dizzy Gillespie and Charlie Parker. Although these concerts were criticized for over-emphasizing the more spectacular, crowd-pleasing aspects of jazz, they did introduce be-bop to a much wider audience.

Some older musicans – Louis Armstrong among them – rejected bop completely. The majority, however, welcomed the introduction of new ideas.

> "Those guys have wonderful minds. It must be wonderful to be pioneers like they are . . . and the funny thing is that it used to be that fifteeen out of twenty people couldn't understand their music and didn't like it. Now if people don't hear it, they wonder what's wrong."
> (Count Basie)

During the 'fifties, there was a revival of interest in New Orleans jazz. It is interesting to note that the only black musicians who took part in this were survivors from the original period of the music. Although a large number of white "trad jazz" bands had considerable commercial success, few serious jazz musicians wanted to put the clock back. The ideas which had seemed so revolutionary in the early 'forties had become an accepted element of jazz by the 'fifties.

Cool jazz

In the earliest days of jazz, the term "hot" was used to describe exciting music. During the 'fifties, there was a reaction against the nervous excitement of bop and the word "cool" was the obvious choice of name for a new style of jazz in which calmness and detachment were the main features.

The most important figure in the development of cool jazz – arguably the most important jazz musician in the last thirty years – was MILES DAVIS. He was born in Alton, Illinois, in 1926 and in 1945 he went to New York to study music at the Juilliard Academy. However, he soon gave this up in favour of jamming at the jazz clubs on 52nd Street. Between 1946 and 1948, he recorded frequently with Charlie Parker. In 1948 he formed a band of his own for a two-week engagement at a club called The Royal Roost. Although only in existence for two weeks, this band was to change the course of jazz history. The line-up consisted of trumpet, trombone, alto and baritone saxes, French horn, tuba, piano, bass and drums. Working with the arranger GIL EVANS, Davis produced music which was quiet and subdued, with an emphasis on technical perfection. In 1949 and 1950, recordings made by this band were released under the title "The Birth of the Cool".

Davis collaborated with Evans again in 1957. The band was bigger this time. It had the conventional trumpet and trombone sections, but the usual saxophone section was replaced by a line-up of alto sax, clarinet, flute, French horn and tuba. In 1958 Davis and Evans released an album of music from Gershwin's "Porgy and Bess". Apart from the unusual instrumental combinations in these recordings, the most distinctive feature is the sound of Davis's trumpet. His tone has almost no vibrato or attack, with notes seeming to emerge from nowhere. Davis made great use of mutes, not the wah-wah and plunger mutes favoured by earlier jazz trumpeters, but the Harmon mute, which produces a quiet, almost muffled, tone.

For Davis, "cool" was more than a style of playing; it was an attitude to life. He was not prepared to make the compromises which earlier jazz musicians had made in order to get work. He saw himself first and foremost as an artist, not an entertainer. He was often criticized for playing with his back to the audience. When asked about this in an interview published in *Melody Maker*, he retorted, "What should I do? Smile at 'em?"

The other major figure in the development of cool jazz was a blind, white pianist from Chicago called LENNIE TRISTANO. In 1951, he founded his "New School of Music" in New York. Tristano's style was very much in the tradition of European classical music – too much so for many critics, who complained that it was "cold" rather than "cool".

The centre of cool jazz moved to America's West Coast, where many musicians combined work in the Hollywood studio orchestras with playing in small jazz groups. Most of the major figures of this so-called West Coast style were white – the saxophonists GERRY MULLIGAN and JIMMY GIUFFRE, the pianists BILL EVANS and DAVE BRUBECK and the drummer SHELLY MANNE. Black musicians included THE MODERN JAZZ QUARTET and the composer and arranger QUINCY JONES. The Modern Jazz Quartet (or MJQ as it was generally known) was founded in 1951 by the pianist JOHN LEWIS. The other members were MILT JACKSON on the vibraphone, PERCY HEATH on bass and the drummer CONNIE KAY. Lewis was particularly influenced by the compositions of J.S. Bach and made great use of the fugue form. In a fugue, each part, or "voice", enters in turn with the initial melody ("subject") and when it finishes takes up the second melody ("counter-subject"). In a four-part fugue, the second and fourth voices enter a fifth above the first and third.

---

vibraphone: *a kind of electric xylophone.*

The success of the MJQ led to a whole series of "jazz fugues" during the 'fifties. In France, the pianist JACQUES LOUSSIER and the vocal group LES SWINGLES went one step further and performed the music of Bach as written, apart from the addition of bass and drums.

For many black musicians, however, cool jazz was moving too far from its roots. In contrast with the "classical" approach of the West Coast a modern version of be-bop developed in New York.

Hard bop

"I don't care who buys the records as long as they get to black people so I will be remembered when I die. I'm not playing for any white people, man, I wanna hear a black guy say, 'Yeah, I dig Miles Davis.'"
(Miles Davis interviewed for *Melody Maker*)

The development of hard bop was part of a social and political revolution in America's black community which began during the 'fifties. Particularly important was the influence of the Black Muslims or, to give them their proper title, the Nation of Islam. They believed that Islam, not Christianity, was the true religion of black Americans and wanted to establish a separate black nation within America. A number of jazz musicians, among them the drummer ART BLAKEY, became Muslims, and their music reflected a pride in black traditions. Many of them adopted Muslim names. Art Blakey was known for a while as Abdullah Ibn Buhaina, while the saxophone player William Evans became YUSEF LATEEF.

▲
With the growth of the Civil Rights movement, many black jazz musicians felt that they should not be looking towards European music for inspiration.

Muslims at prayer in a New York temple. ▶

Hard bop extended the harmonic experiments of be-bop, but it was much more fiercely rhythmic, almost aggressive. The two most important group leaders were both drummers, Blakey and MAX ROACH. Blakey was deeply interested in African music, and visited Africa in the early 'fifties. On his return to the United States he put together several "drum orchestras", using both African and Cuban musicians alongside jazz drummers. He is best-known, however, for his work with THE JAZZ MESSENGERS. Over the years, this group, under Blakey's leadership, has been a training school for a host of fine jazz musicians.

While cool jazz looked to European classical music for inspiration, hard bop turned to black American traditions, such as blues and gospel. The pianist HORACE SILVER developed a style of playing medium-tempo blues pieces with a heavy beat, to which the label "funky" was given. In fact, the words "funk" and "soul" were both first used in jazz during the 'fifties, before they became more general terms for black popular music.

In 1955, Miles Davis formed a hard bop quintet which introduced another new element into jazz. Since the earliest days, jazz musicians had improvised around the underlying chords of tunes. Davis, and the tenor saxophonist JOHN COLTRANE, however, began to experiment with the use of modes instead. This was the system of scales which was used in European music from the Middle Ages until the sixteenth century. A similar system is also used in Indian classical music, where the modes are known as ragas. Each mode starts on a different note and, while each has five intervals of a tone and two of a semi-tone, the semi-tones occur in different places depending upon the starting note. Each mode therefore has its own particular character – this can be heard by playing a series of scales on a piano, using only the white notes.

The use of modes gave jazz musicians greater freedom for improvisation, since they were no longer limited by the need to stick to predetermined chord changes. It also prepared the way for the next development – "free jazz".

Free jazz

As the name implies, free jazz broke away from the "rules" of rhythm and harmony which jazz musicians had generally followed. It introduced elements from other musical cultures – notably those of Asia and North Africa – and re-explored such Afro-American musical traditions as field hollers, blues and gospel. The gospel element was particularly important, with many musicians adopting a musical equivalent of "speaking in tongues". Many free jazz recordings had all the fervour of an evangelical prayer meeting. Accepted ideas about what could be called jazz – or even what could be called music – were pushed to the limit. Jazz had ceased to be a branch of popular music with the advent of be-bop, but now it became a vehicle for expressing political and religious feelings as well as musical ideas.

The development of free jazz is closely linked with the careers of two saxophone players – JOHN COLTRANE (tenor) and ORNETTE COLEMAN (alto). Coltrane was born in North Carolina in 1926. His first professional engagement was in 1947, when he worked with the blues singer BIG MAYBELLE. This was followed by spells with several other blues-based bands before he joined Miles Davis in 1955. It was with Davis, with whom he stayed until 1960, that

---

evangelical: *Christian sects which emphasize the importance of personally experiencing the power of God. Their services often involve "speaking in tongues", the use of unknown "languages". The "gift of tongues" was given to Christ's disciples at Whitsun (Pentecost). Christians believe it was the Holy Spirit speaking through them, while onlookers thought they had drunk too much wine.*

◀ *The modal jazz developed by Miles Davis and John Coltrane led to an interest in Indian music. During the 1960s and 1970s many Indian musicians toured in the West, often appearing on the same platform as rock and jazz musicians.*

Coltrane began to experiment in the use of modes. He also developed a technique which came to be known as "sheets of sound", notes following each other so quickly that they had the effect of a piano player rapidly striking different chords with the sustaining pedal held down.

In 1960, he formed his own group and gained a large following with his interpretation, on the soprano saxophone, of "My Favourite Things". He took this simple waltz from the musical *The Sound of Music* and turned it into one of the finest examples of extended improvisation ever recorded. His ability to make something of the simplest melodies was also revealed in his treatment of "Greensleeves". He began to develop an interest in Arabic and Indian music and gradually moved away from the European ideas of harmony which had dominated jazz.

He was a deeply religious man, and in 1964 he recorded what is generally regarded as his greatest work, "A Love Supreme". In 1957 he had experienced "through the grace of God", as he said, "a spiritual awakening". "A Love Supreme" was the result of this, a prayer in which Coltrane used his saxophone to express what he could not express with his voice. The whole piece, divided into four parts, is built upon a single chord. It was followed by other religious works, "Meditations" and "Ascension", each relying more and more upon free improvisation. Coltrane poured his soul into his music in a way that no other musician had ever done. At the end of each public performance he would be physically exhausted, and during the 'sixties he had to take frequent breaks from playing. He died in 1967 and although the cause of death was diagnosed as a liver complaint, the emotional intensity of his music must have taken its toll.

Ornette Coleman, born in Texas in 1930, lacked Coltrane's musical background. He was a self-taught musician and learnt to play the alto saxophone without realizing that it is a transposing instrument – in other words, an E♭ on the alto sounds the same

as a C on the piano. Other musicians did not like working with him, claiming that he played out of tune. When he was in a blues band led by PEE WEE CRAYTON, Crayton actually paid him not to play! Unable to make a living from music, Coleman took a job as a lift operator in Los Angeles, stopping his lift on the top floor during quiet spells to practise his saxophone and study harmony. Eventually, he found a musician prepared to work with him. DON CHERRY was an equally unorthodox character, who used a pocket trumpet instead of the standard kind. Coleman meanwhile had found that he preferred the tone of a plastic alto saxophone. Whereas John Coltrane moved gradually towards free-form jazz, Coleman jumped straight in. He developed a system of harmony which he called "harmolodics", which was based primarily on melody rather than the idea of a tune being in a particular key. This gave

soloists the freedom to improvise without having to keep to a pre-arranged chord pattern.

In 1961, he released his most influential album, "Free Jazz". It consisted of a free improvisation by a double quartet. Coleman's own quartet was joined by another led by ERIC DOLPHY on bass clarinet. The only limits agreed upon were the order of the solos and the length of time the session should last. The musicians, of course, did not just play anything they felt like. It was a collective improvisation, with each player listening to and blending in with the others.

Other musicians followed Coleman's lead, producing music by comparison with which the "Free Jazz" album sounds like "easy listening"! Saxophonists such as PHAROAH SANDERS, ALBERT AYLER and ARCHIE SHEPP broke all the "rules" about what their instrument should sound like.

Shepp described his saxophone as a machine gun, his music as an attack on an American government which was waging war in Vietnam. He was not the only one to use his music to make political statements. Opposition to the Vietnam War and support for the Black Muslims and the Civil Rights movement all influenced jazz musicians of the period.

◀ *American soldiers in Vietnam and National Guardsmen in riot-torn Washington. The jazz of the late 'sixties reflected the times in which it was created.*
▼

Not all the jazz of this era was angry or militant, however. Much of it displays the fascination with Eastern religions and philosophy which was a feature of the 'sixties. There was also a renewed interest in black folk music. Musicians such as CHARLES MINGUS, ERIC DOLPHY and ROLAND KIRK combined many different aspects of Afro-American culture in their music. Kirk, who died in 1975, was one of the strangest characters to emerge from the world of jazz. As a child he had been accidentally blinded by a nurse who was treating his eyes. Despite this tragedy, his music was noteworthy for its humour. He was a multi-instrumentalist, often playing two or three instruments at the same time. As well as the saxophone, he also played the flute

Much free jazz was influenced by the music of Muslim Africa.

and two old-fashioned Spanish reed instruments, the stritch and the manzello.

The use of unusual instruments was a feature of the jazz of this period. The soprano saxophone, for example, had almost entirely gone out of fashion after the days of New Orleans jazz. Following on from John Coltrane, however, a large number of musicians began to use it because of its "African" sound. At the other extreme, the unwieldy bass saxophone was used as a solo instrument by ROSCOE MITCHELL. Eric Dolphy preferred the more velvety sound of the bass clarinet, while YUSEF LATEEF experimented with the oboe and bassoon. Don Cherry has used wind instruments from many parts of the world, including Tibet, India and China. Even the bagpipes, in their North African rather than Scottish form, have been used for jazz.

Free jazz was not a commercially successful form of music. Many more traditionally-minded jazz fans felt that it was merely a way for inferior musicians to hide their inability to play "properly". Record companies were also put off by its political overtones. In the early 'sixties, an organization known as the ASSOCIATION FOR THE ADVANCEMENT OF CREATIVE MUSICIANS (AACM) was established in Chicago. Its aim was to publicize the work of black musicians and to provide a means of sharing ideas. The word "jazz" is rather limiting when applied to the music of such AACM groups as THE ART ENSEMBLE OF CHICAGO and THE WORLD SAXOPHONE QUARTET. Instead, the Art Ensemble referred to what they played as "great black music".

PART FIVE

ELECTRIC JAZZ

Jazz musicians have used electrical means to make instruments louder since the 'thirties. The development of the electric guitar, for instance, enabled it to become a front-line instrument rather than a member of the rhythm section. Electricity can be used to do more than amplify instruments, however. It can also be used to alter their sound, to create effects which cannot be produced on an acoustic instrument. Generally speaking, it was left to rock musicians to explore these possibilities.

During the 'sixties, rock music also began to display an increasing jazz influence. In Britain, there was a fashion for various styles of black American popular music, generally grouped together under the label "rhythm and blues" (R & B). British R & B groups included many musicians who had a jazz background, and they formed the nucleus of what came to be known as the "progressive" rock groups of the late 'sixties. Although there was much talk of a fusion of rock and jazz, the music of these groups was very old-fashioned in jazz terms. As with some of the dance bands of the 'twenties, jazz musicians added a little spice without changing the basic nature of the music. In the United States there were several attempts to create rock big bands – BLOOD, SWEAT AND TEARS and CHICAGO, for example – but these were generally shortlived.

Of far more importance was the career of the guitarist JIMI HENDRIX. Although labelled as a rock musician, he had much in common with free-form jazz pioneers such as John Coltrane and Ornette Coleman. Like them, he served an apprenticeship in the backing bands of blues-based singers and his playing always retained this blues influence. He was born in Seattle in 1947 and died in London in 1970. Though his life was so short, he revolutionized electric guitar technique, using the instrument as a switch to turn on a dazzling array of electronic effects. His music displayed the full range of emotions, from tenderness to anger, in a way that no other rock musician had ever managed before. Shortly before his death, plans were made for Hendrix to work with the jazz composer and arranger Gil Evans. Evans, it will be remembered, had collaborated with Miles Davis in the 'fifties, and it was Davis who made the great breakthrough in the fusion of jazz and rock.

In 1970, he released "Bitches Brew", the first really successful jazz-rock album. The group line-up included two electric pianos and electric guitar, but even more startling was the trumpet technique which Davis employed. A pick-up was attached to the mouthpiece of the instrument, connecting it to an amplifier. This allowed Davis to use

---

amplify: *to make louder.*

---

acoustic: *without electrical aplification.*

R & B: *rhythm and blues. This was a phrase originally used by American record companies in the 'forties and 'fifties to describe popular music produced by black musicians and aimed at black audiences.*

devices, such as the wah-wah pedal, previously employed only by guitarists. Several members of groups led by Davis in this period went on to form jazz-rock groups of their own. They included the pianists CHICK COREA, HERBIE HANCOCK and JOE ZAWINUL and the guitarist JOHN McLAUGHLIN. Zawinul's WEATHER REPORT was the most commercially successful of these groups. Davis himself moved away from rock towards funk, the rhythmic element of his music becoming increasingly important.

Ornette Coleman also moved in a similar direction, combining free-form improvisation with funk rhythms. Increasingly, the dividing line between jazz and funk has become blurred. At one extreme, there is the smooth sound of GEORGE BENSON and GROVER WASHINGTON JUNIOR, while at the other is the aggressive "new wave" music of JAMES BLOOD ULMER and trombonist LESTER BOWIES's band DEFUNKT.

Jazz-rock was fairly shortlived, but jazz-funk has lasted much longer. This is hardly surprising, as jazz and soul share the same roots. Jazz musicians have always had close links with other forms of black popular music and, for much of its history, jazz has also been dance music.

"Right from the start, musical reactionaries have said the worst about bop. But after seing the Savoy Ballroom kids fit dances to this kind of music, I felt it was destined to become the new era of music."
(Mary Lou Williams)

It is interesting that Mary Lou Williams defended bop against its critics by saying that it could be danced to, whereas many modern critics look down on jazz-funk for that same reason. During the 'fifties and 'sixties, jazz became, in the words of John Storm Roberts, "an 'art' music, no longer a 'people' music". Since the early 'seventies, jazz has increasingly become a "people" music once again.

There are several jazz compositions whose titles neatly sum up what jazz is all about:

"It Don't Mean A Thing If It Ain't Got That Swing."
(Duke Ellington)

"'Tain't What Ya Do, It's The Way That Ya Do It."
(Jimmy Lunceford)

In the 'eighties, the guitarist James Blood Ulmer added a new one to the list:

"Jazz Is The Teacher, Funk Is The Preacher."

---

wah-wah pedal: *a foot pedal which triggers a rapid alteration between the extremes of the treble and bass controls on an amplifier. This produces a distinctive "wah-wah" sound.*

---

funk: *Originally black slang for sweat, the word was adopted as a descriptive term for emotionally intense blues or soul music.*

---

reactionary: *a person who dislikes change.*

CONCLUSION

Since the turn of the century, a new style of jazz has emerged roughly every ten years. No new style has emerged in the 'eighties, but there has been a consolidation of what has gone before. The free jazz experiments of the 'sixties are continuing, while bop and its descendants have become the new "mainstream". New Orleans-style jazz and big band Swing both have their devoted followers. The popularity of jazz-funk has led to a renewed interest in earlier styles, as well as to an interest in Latin American and African music.

Although this book has been concerned with developments in the United States, jazz has become a world music, not confined to one particular country. Right from the earliest days, jazz was popular in Europe, particularly in France, which has been referred to as "the second country of jazz". Many black American jazz musicians made their homes in France, Sidney Bechet, in particular, becoming as much a part of the French entertainment world as Edith Piaf or Maurice Chevalier. With few exceptions, however, European jazz musicians were content to follow American trends rather than developing their own styles. The free jazz movement of the 'sixties changed this, as musicians began to look to different cultures for inspiration. The term "jazz" became as much an attitude of mind as a definition of a particular type of music. In eastern Europe and South Africa, jazz musicians are often at the forefront of the struggle for political freedom.

In western Europe and America, jazz has once more become a form of popular music after a long period in which it was relegated to small clubs and late-night radio programmes. It is fitting that the most successful jazz artist of the 'eighties, WYNTON MARSALIS, should come from New Orleans, for too long regarded as little more than a jazz museum. Marsalis is equally well-known for his performances of classical trumpet music and is in the tradition of virtuoso jazz soloists which stretches back to Louis Armstrong. At the same time, there is a growing number of young musicians in New Orleans who look back to an even older tradition – the collective improvisation of the marching bands. The best-known of these is THE DIRTY DOZEN BRASS BAND. Their music is not some sort of New Orleans "revival", but modern band music. The band has a traditional line-up – including two drummers, one playing snare drum, the other bass – but the music is a mixture of popular tunes, brass band standards and wild free-form blowing. A phrase from Kalamu ya Salaam's sleevenotes to their album "Mardi Grass In Montreaux: Live" serves as an excellent conclusion to a book about jazz:

"This is new/old wonderful, timeless black dance music."

---

snare drum: *a drum in which the lower head has a set of wires attached. These vibrate when the upper head is struck.*

King Oliver's Jazz Band, 1922. Oliver, fifth from the left, was the first black jazz musician to make a record. The young Louis Armstrong is standing next to him.

GLOSSARY OF MUSICAL TERMS

bar   a group of beats, the first of which is generally stressed (emphasized). The number of beats in a bar is indicated by the TIME SIGNATURE.

beat   a regular pulse.

chord   a group of three or more notes sounded together. The series of chords which accompanies a melody is known as a chord progression. It is possible to fit new melodies to such a series of chords.

counterpoint   a form of music in which two or more melodies sound at the same time. The horizontal movement of parts is more important than the vertical structure of chords.

harmony   a combination of musical sounds. The chords which accompany a tune.

key   A piece of music is often said to be "in" a particular key. This means that the notes of the major scale with that name will be used. The melody will generally finish on the starting note of that scale. Notes which do not belong to that scale can also be used to add extra colour.
They are known as CHROMATIC notes, after the Greek word for colour.
    During the nineteenth century composers made increasing use of such notes. Their harmony was no longer based on major and minor scales and became known as CHROMATIC HARMONY.
    During the twentieth century, a system was developed which gave all twelve notes of the chromatic scale equal importance, doing away with the idea of key altogether.

rhythm   different combinations of stresses and sound lengths made into a pattern.

slur   an unbroken move from one note to another.

syncopation   placing an accent on the normally unstressed beats of a bar, or playing whole groups of notes which clash with the underlying beat.

theme   a short melody. The main musical idea of a piece, around which variations can be written or improvised.

tone   this has two different meanings: (i) an interval of two semi-tones; (ii) the quality of sound produced by an individual musician. It is also used sometimes to mean TIMBRE. This is the sound produced by a particular instrument. (For example, the violin has a different timbre from the trumpet.)

unison   several musicians playing the same tune together, without using any harmony.

vibrato   a slight, rapid alteration in the pitch of a note. A kind of controlled "wobble".

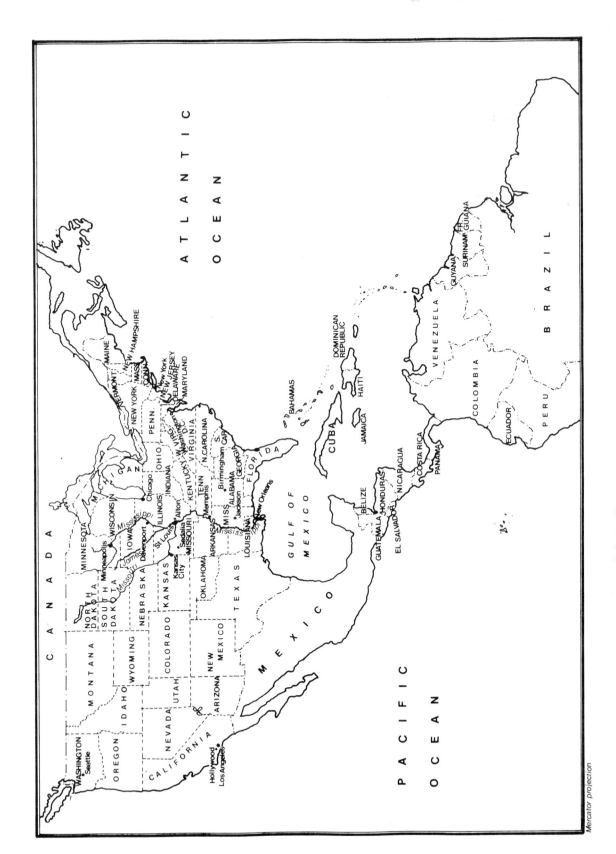

Mercator projection

DATE LIST

1776 – American Declaration of Independence
1861 – American Civil War
1863 – Abolition of slavery in the United States
1914 – Outbreak of First World War
1917 – U.S.A. enters war
1918 – End of First World War
1920 – Introduction of Prohibition
1929 – Wall Street Crash – start of the Depression
1933 – End of Prohibition
1939 – Outbreak of Second World War
1941 – Japanese attack Pearl Harbor – United States enters the war
1945 – End of Second World War
1950 – Korean War (armistice signed 1953)
1959 – Cuban Revolution
1961 – United States backs unsuccessful invasion of Cuba
1963 – Beginning of the Civil Rights movement
     – Assassination of John F. Kennedy

1964 – Three civil rights workers murdered in Mississippi
     – U.S. bombing of North Vietnam
1965 – American troops sent to South Vietnam
     – Assassination of Malcolm X
1967 – Rioting in several American cities
1968 – Assassination of Doctor Martin Luther King
1969 – First moon landing
1971 – Attica Prison riot – forty people killed
1973 – Last American soldiers leave Vietnam
1974 – Resignation of President Nixon after Watergate scandal
1975 – End of Vietnam War – the longest war in the twentieth century
1977 – President Carter pardons Vietnam War "draft dodgers"

DISCOGRAPHY

Jazz records are constantly being deleted and re-issued, so the accuracy of the following list cannot be guaranteed. (Thanks to Martin Salisbury of the Record Trade Centre in Beckenham for his assistance.)

Roots of jazz

AFRICAN JOURNEY: VOLUMES 1 & 2 – Sonet – SNTF 666/667
"MARCHING ALONG" – EASTMAN SYMPHONIC WIND ENSEMBLE – Mercury Golden Imports – SRI 75004
  (Side one of this record consists of Sousa marches in their original arrangements.)
"ELLA SINGS GERSHWIN" – ELLA FITZGERALD – MCA 1820
"STREETS OF GOLD" – THE KLEZMORIM – Arhoolie 3011

THE SOUL OF BLACK MUSIC: VOLUMES 1 & 2 — Sonet — SNTF 795/6
STORY OF THE BLUES — CBS 22135
PIANO RAGS BY SCOTT JOPLIN — JOSHUA RIFKIN — Nonesuch — H 71248 & H 71264

Styles of jazz
JAZZ CLASSICS IN DIGITAL STEREO — B.B.C. Records
VOLUME ONE — NEW ORLEANS — REB 588
VOLUME TWO — CHICAGO — REB 589
VOLUME THREE — NEW YORK — REB 590
JELLY ROLL MORTON — THE KING OF NEW ORLEANS JAZZ — RCA — INTS 5092
THE LOUIS ARMSTRONG LEGEND — EMI — SH 404
THE INDISPENSABLE BIX BEIDERBECKE — RCA — NL 89572
DUKE ELLINGTON — COTTON CLUB DAYS — RCA — CL 89801
DUKE ELLINGTON — GREATEST HITS — CBS — 21059
COUNT BASIE — SWINGING THE BLUES — Affinity — AFS 1010
THE GREAT BIG BANDS — Disques Festival — ALB 371 (Dist. Musidisc Europe)
CHARLIE PARKER/DIZZY GILLESPIE — EMI — 2M 056 64847
JAZZ AT THE PHILHARMONIC 1949 — Verve — VRV 5
SLIM GAILLARD — THE VOUTEST — Hep — HEP 28
MILES DAVIES — THE BIRTH OF THE COOL — Capitol — TC CAPS 1024
ART BLAKEY — A NIGHT AT BIRDLAND — Blue Note — BST 81521
THE BEST OF BLUE NOTE — VOLUMES ONE & TWO — Blue Note — BST2 84429/33
JOHN COLTRANE — THE ART OF — Atlantic — K 60052
ORNETTE COLMAN — FREE JAZZ — Atlantic — ATL 50240
ROLAND KIRK — NOW PLEASE DON'T YOU CRY, BEAUTIFUL EDITH — Verve — 2304 519
CANNONBALL ADDERLEY — ACCENT ON AFRICA — Affinity — AFF 148
MILES DAVIS — BITCHES' BREW — CBS — 66236
WEATHER REPORT — 8.30 — CBS — 22134
HERBIE HANCOCK — FUTURE SHOCK — CBS — 25540
CHARLIE HADEN — THE BALLAD OF THE FALLEN — ECM — 1248
WYNTON MARSALIS — BLACK CODES (FROM THE UNDERGROUND) CBS — 26686
DIRTY DOZEN BRASS BAND — MARDI GRAS IN MONTREUX. LIVE. — Rounder Europa — REU 1009

INDEX